# The Wilderness Within

Barbara Spring

PublishAmerica
Baltimore

© 2003 by Barbara Spring.
All rights reserved. No part of this book may be reproduced in any form without written permission from the publishers, except by a reviewer who may quote brief passages in a review to be printed in a newspaper or magazine.

First printing

ISBN: 1-59286-785-5
PUBLISHED BY PUBLISHAMERICA, LLLP
www.publishamerica.com
Baltimore

Printed in the United States of America

*To Norm*

*my traveling companion*

Barbara Spring is the author of *The Dynamic Great Lakes*, a nonfiction book about changes in the Great Lakes ecosystem.

# *Acknowledgments*

My mentors have given me so much over the years. My first poetry teacher was A.J.M. Smith, Poet Laureate of Canada, from whom I took classes at M.S.U. I have also studied poetry in several workshops with Robert Bly; the U.S. Poet Laureate Wm. Stafford; Pulitzer Prize winner N. Scott Momaday and Coleman Barks, poet and collector of words. I am grateful to all of my teachers. They have enriched my life.

I am grateful to my friends and family who have taught me, supported me and given me so much good material.

## *Pictures*

Inuit sculpture of polar bear that was part
of the Master's of the Arctic exhibition
sponsored by the United Nations.  17

Photo of a salmon in a clear stream.  26

Prehistoric cave painting of a standing bison.
Altamira, Spain.  43

Photo of a Tarahumara woman.
Copper Canyon, Mexico, 2000.  64

Massacio's Expulsion of Adam and Eve, 1425,
Fresco. Santa Maria del Carmine, Florence, Italy.  76

Face of the Green Man in a Gothic Cathedral
Window.  80

Photo of a diatom taken through an electron
microscope.  93

*Contents*

| | |
|---|---|
| Bear Woman | 17 |
| North | 18 |
| Safe in the Universe | 18 |
| Wolfman | 19 |
| Unseen Singer, Haiku | 20 |
| Tracks, Tanka | 20 |
| Frog Pond, Haiku | 20 |
| Ruby Throat | 21 |
| Bedtime Story | 22 |
| The Library at Alexandria | 23 |
| A Small Gift for You | 24 |
| Celtic Mirror | 25 |
| Circuits | 26 |
| Easter Morning | 27 |
| In May | 27 |
| Stormy May Morning | 28 |
| Migrations | 29 |
| Two Horses | 29 |
| Whale Songs | 30 |
| My Strawberries | 31 |
| The Hero's Journey | 32 |
| Persephone Emerges | 33 |
| Lake Michigan Aubade | 35 |
| Summer Solstice | 36 |
| Maybe the Manitous | 37 |
| Moon | 38 |
| Snow | 39 |

| | |
|---|---|
| Aubade | 39 |
| Bloodroot Bearings | 40 |
| Meditation | 41 |
| At Palisades Nuclear Power Plant | 41 |
| Bats | 42 |
| The Gatherer | 42 |
| The Hunter | 43 |
| My Deer | 44 |
| The Effects of Moon Chimes Upon Deer and Other Sublunary Beings | 45 |
| The Ancestors | 46 |
| Praise | 47 |
| Day Lily | 48 |
| My Kites for My Father | 49 |
| On Puget Sound | 50 |
| Whale Dreams | 51 |
| Night Realities | 52 |
| La Mer | 52 |
| Lost Found Fawn | 53 |
| Prairie Child | 54 |
| In Darkness | 55 |
| Birth Control for the Earth Mother Rampant Upon a Fruitful World | 56 |
| Sophia's Gold | 58 |
| Mexico | 59 |
| Ix Chel | 59 |
| Dzbilchaltun | 60 |
| In the Cenote | 61 |
| Copper Canyon and the Tarahumara Indians | 62 |
| Tarahumara Newborn | 65 |
| My Baby | 66 |
| Queen Asa's Viking Ship | 67 |

| | |
|---|---|
| Refuge | 68 |
| Variations | 68 |
| Galapagos | 69 |
| What Charles Darwin Saw (Essay) | 69 |
| Overboard | 72 |
| Floreana | 73 |
| Isla Espanola | 74 |
| Where Have All the Goddesses Gone? | 76 |
| Hieros Gamos | 77 |
| Holy Bones | 78 |
| Agate, A Gate | 78 |
| The Green Man's Secret | 79 |
| Dark Rib Ride | 81 |
| Shopping for a Drum | 82 |
| Denali Spring Time | 83 |
| Canadian Geese | 84 |
| He Was a Farm Boy Once | 85 |
| Wild Flowers | 85 |
| High School Library | 86 |
| Wordless Song | 87 |
| Foggy Dawn | 87 |
| Bonesounds | 88 |
| The Monarchs' Wedding | 89 |
| Song in the Flesh | 90 |
| Radial Lines | 90 |
| Sophia's Sound | 91 |
| Mist | 92 |
| Dark Energy | 93 |
| Unseen Opals | 93 |
| Great Lakes Give and Take | 94 |
| Great Lakes Imprint On Us | 95 |
| Great Yin Mother | 96 |

| | |
|---|---|
| Snowy Owls | 97 |
| To Daughters and Sons | 98 |
| The Entryway | 99 |
| Equation | 100 |
| Africa | 101 |
| In a Nyala's Eye | 101 |
| At Victoria Falls | 102 |
| I Still Hear the Roar of the Falls | 104 |
| Riding the Spirit Elephant | 106 |
| Seaspeak | 107 |
| Abyss | 108 |
| Dawn Dragons | 109 |
| Mt. St. Helens Blooms | 109 |
| Basic Instincts | 110 |
| Jonah's Journey, Sonnet | 111 |
| Eric Our Guide Shows Us Santa Croce | 112 |
| Dante's Limerick | 113 |
| Twin Sewing Lessons | 114 |
| Forget Me Nots and Otters | 115 |
| The Gift of Rabbit | 116 |

## *Introduction*

They just keep coming, these poems. Some poems arrive from mysterious places; dreams or wide-awake reveries take me places I have never been before. Many enter in from the Great Lakes region where I live. Others come home with me in my suitcase after traveling. I have included some travel stories that go with certain poems.

Places, friends, family, animals, birds, fish, flowers, stones, lakes, rivers—and the unseen world enter these poems in unexpected ways. All of these weave together into the fabric of life itself. These poems shimmer at the threshold where inner and outer worlds meet.

## *Bear Woman*

The grizzly terrified us at first—
pacing the driveway with her three cubs,
battering at our front door.
She terrifies you now;
you can see her in my eyes.

So I've trained her as Gypsies do:
I beat a tambourine,
force her to walk on hot embers.

She rises,
lifts one hind foot,
then the other.

She dances to my tambourine.

## North

Astride the ice bear I ride:
I hold handfuls of his hollow hair
hands knees heels clasp
his rocking gait.
Arctic winds sculpt
the ellipse of his shape.

Our long blue shadow rides on the east.
We hear seals who sing
under fast ice.

## Safe in the Universe

Light surrounds me
in the dark

my radiant Sophia
everywhere.

Guardians at my threshold
black and white bears.

## *Wolfman*

All night his wheels roll
through the woods.
He shines his light.
He shoots
the deer we had been feeding.

When he was born his mother
toothed the sac and
he heard the stream by his window
speak to him in tongues.
His yellow eyes opened and
through a crack in the roof
he learned the trick of changing
with the waxing moon.

As soon as he could walk
she chased him out of the house.
He learned to run down rabbits.

Now no woman can keep him
at home. He paces then escapes
to rural cross
roads, the bracken, the swamp.

## Unseen Singer

Eager for first light
one unseen singer blesses
the sleepless with song.

## Tracks

The wild turkeys run—
they leave runic calligraphy
in the forest trail we follow.
We hold our breaths and listen.

## Frog Pond

A madcap chorus
sings of mud moonbeams and love
all the frog long night.

### Ruby Throat

The hummingbird darts
as a watch fob swings
bejeweled plumb-bob
on a golden string
his wings a blur
his clockwork parts
cut backward forward
pendulum arcs.

He shivers blue silk
splinters the light
the shards sing and shine
in his courtship flight.

# Bedtime Story

Bako.
Yes?
Tell me about the pterodactyls.

Once when the Spirit moved across the face of the waters,
pterodactyls sliced the skin of twilight.
Their scimitar wings would glide over fern filigrees,
their silent shadows would slide over still oceans
and over hills still curled like newborns below.

When Heaven and Earth were new,
pterosaurs soared through warm air,
sea monsters swarmed and sang.

Did they eat little girls?

No, no, no. They swam in their sea cradle.
The pterosaurs soared.
The little girls looked down from Heaven
and God said it was very good.

But now I'm here in my bed.
Where are the pterodactyls?

No 50-foot shadow will darken your bed.
All the pterodactyls are dead—imbedded in stone.
Their hollow bones once one with the wind
lie among impressions of raindrops,
distillations of ferns,
insects caught in amber

and fossilized footprints of terrified lizards.

Bako.
Yes?
I can't sleep.

## *The Library at Alexandria*
### *for Robert Bly*

Bearing a jumble of dusty objects
dredged from the ashes deep core,
he hastens toward me, he

accessed what had been forbidden before:
an armload of curious things, things I had asked for
since the age of seven.

What I received awakens the dark horses
who raise their heads
and look into my eyes like newborns.

## *A Small Gift For You*

If I were to serve a medieval feast to you
on Parisian golden platters for the king
of wild game, spiced wine in jeweled goblets,
we'd have dominion over all.

If the fragrance of crushed leaves and odor
of forest floor should cling to us now
we could change into oaks and live for centuries
with roots and branches intertwined.

If I could paint a masterpiece
of a daisy dappled and harebell shadowed
high mountain meadow in the early morning light
we'd lie together for timeless hours.

If I could murmur the sound of rivers
and roll thunder out my throat
the walls of Jericho would
fall at my shout.
If my envelope of skin should touch
the margins of the earth
and my spirit fly, I could tell you
of the roll and pitching of the sky.

But if I gave myself to you
as a child gives a small gift
would you accept me with a smile
and not deny?

## *Celtic Mirror*

When seasons change
and migrations flow through air and water
I long for my home.

When I'm alone
at high noon with full moon, I find our thoughts
entwined: two vines

incised on ancient stone
where two minds find their homeland
and a river runs underground

where birds with bright blue feathers
delight us with their sounds.

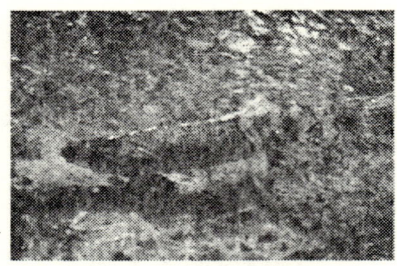

## *Circuits*

Light from a star that died
    shines out
from jade green eyes.

A salmon tail fans streambed stones
    and dark silt swirls.

Millennia ago a star spurt fire and
    now a constellation of eggs
    and white milt spiral down
    in black water.

Fishbone lattices litter the stream
    that speaks of glaciers
    and purls.

Frost flowers bloom on the cut bank
while embryos curl in sweet cold sleep below.

## *Easter Morning*

As I walked out this morning
I found two halves of a speckled egg
on the ground. I found an empty cocoon
spun of finest silk thread.
And then I trembled when I saw the empty
tomb of my Teacher.
As I turned, I heard the reedy cheeps
of four flightless nestlings
a luna moth floated
past my vision.

This morning Jesus walked with me
and how my heart burned within me
when I heard all he spoke.

## *In May*

Each green gothic leaf
burns blush red
as young girls at first
communion.

Each clench-fisted fern
bursts the sod
wears a bronze hair shirt
waits and prays.

Each blueberry bush
with waxen bells
ring silent peals
bees hear.

A kind of shining
floods the woods
as Heaven brings in May.

## *Stormy May Morning*

From the Great Lakes to Texas
great sounds of thunder, splashes of rain
soak thirsty dune grasses
all my five senses.
And the five peach
and cream tulips
I planted last fall—
I could lie down in the rain
in the tulips you know.

Listen—the rain patters now
chortles in downspouts
as the sun peeks out.
Orioles splash their citrus arias—
later I'll leave them halves of oranges
flown from Texas.

## *Migrations*

Two Cape May warblers
in the basswood tree
feed amid froths of flowers.
They clean each twig of insects
gather strength for their northward flight.
Silver leaf green notes sift through
filigrees, dimple the steam below.

At night, swept in wind tides with
yellow warblers, blackburnians
and other kin
they flow on again.

## *Two Horses*

Standing so close to each other they almost touch
two white horses near the fence.

I speak to them saying how handsome they are
and the old one strikes a show horse pose
even though he is bony, spavined, swaybacked.

"Oh, you are fine," I say
and he lowers his eyelids at my compliment.

The young horse looks at me with the eyes of a child
on the first day of school.

# *Whale Songs*

First solo then symphonies
echo off me
roll up from lowly troughs
resonate my bones.

And what whales know of sojourns
both land and sea
leave deep longings in me.

And the humpbacks' keenings—
titanic leviathan harmonics
spill from pole to pole
through all holy seas—

they breach to take a look
and one said,

"Woman, why don't you sing to me?"

Then sounding, left a footprint
on the rolling sea.

# *My Straw berries*

In summer there's a lot of scut work to do
the strawberries need picking every day.
The slugs and sow bugs burrow into
the sweetest berries. So I bite
the other red sweet cheeks
where many slug lips
haven't been—I don't
like to share with
slugs and bugs.
I wanted the
best ones
for
me.

## *The Hero's Journey*

The lake's Prussian glaze shimmers
a slight wind fingers
its surface.

Fishermen troll the still deeps
the first day of spring
forgetting

their wives, their children, their homes.
They float on the lake
bundled up

like babies. What if they should
become like still life mezzotints

encased behind frames and glass
or wound up neatly in
skeins of wool

forever in their wives' rooms?
Men should roam the seas
standing up
in their boats to pee in the
water, free to be...
lonesome heroes.

## *Persephone Emerges*

Under willows' first fuzz
Eden green
goats graze
feeding unborn kids.
The warbler haunted woods
flickers green fire—
the river brims a billion suns.

Persephone burst
from under earth covered with leaf mold
and blinking in the fawn spotted dawn
in the cool wooded dunes.

Above her head, flecks of foam
flowers, bloodroot and trillium
splash the dark soil,
spilled milk
at a sacrificial rite.
Persephone emerges.

Morning light veils her body
darts through her jewels
her crown of diamonds, rubies, emeralds.
She carries sweet spring
time in her
with the vision of night.

On the mirror still surface of a lake,
mayflies suffer breech births,
wiggle out of wetsuits

nymphs no longer
and with wings clear as water
they wobble into flight
rise like clouds of smoke
in golden light.

A catbird speaks in tongues
its throat bubbles out ineffable delights.

Bees spin in dusty pollen,
melt water burbles,
rises through red veins of leaves,
Persephone's footprints fill with water.

## *Lake Michigan Aubade*

Mist rises, March morning
a song bird's longing shears moist air,
drifts from thickets.
From empty porches of summer homes
wind chimes play, hollow melodious shards of clay.
And the lake never ceases sounds in March:
ice chunks chink, shards break and break
against the shore.
Waves dash ice against troll caves of ice
and break ice feet.
Mist rises from green briars
where wild birds braid their songs
through tangled skeins
and the blood that rushes through my veins
echoes
the waves
on shore.

## *Summer Solstice*

Birds notes of all colors tumble
through the foggy air
and I can't sleep.

Flowing notes are small colored stones
cascading all through
the foggy dawn.

On the longest day of the year
I wanted to snooze
but sleep eludes.

A parliament of finches sings
a gang of robins
two cardinals drop

their cherry ripe notes into the
doppelganger fog
that magnifies

every jubilant trilling.
Rose breasted grosbeaks
calling catbirds

towhees, wrens, swallows bend their
twittering love songs
percolating

through morning air—gentle doves
mourn while blue jays

jeer rude blue notes.

Summer solstice jolts me awake—
blazons summer on songbird hinges.

## *Maybe the Manitous*

Eastward rolling water
pellucid dense and slow
Karo syrup gloss or
flowing molten glass.

One crystal grabs
one grain of sand and
the beach blooms
with frost flowers—
a stiff white collar grows
all along the sandy shore.

Cold.
Icy winds blast.
Ice balls bob, wink, crash.
An eagle's cry hangs
midair
above a white horizon line—
when sweetwater seas
freeze.

Late afternoon sun—
deep blue shadows on snow

manitous whisper to ice shelves
sibilant spirits speak —
murmur to structures below.

From Milwaukee to Muskegon
cold rollers flow, then splash through
ice volcanoes on the shore
troll caves and canon balls
shot from polar storms…
or maybe the manitous.

## *Moon*

3 A.M.
a full moon blinding me
through my west window.
If I could,
I would fly away

to where scarlet ibis fly
to an island of sweet music.

This morning the lake plankton
rose to the surface to drink moonlight
and the opalescent diatoms
spun for joy
in the bright November light.

Moonlight sheets through my window
reminding me of when I

was 19, 20 and 21.
When I look again
the moon is gone.

## *Snow*

Snow swirls out of an immense
spinning wheel
each six sided shape
a perfect thought of the spinner
untouched as yet by the world.

Snow slants down across
lakes, dunes and a house where
a young girl plays
and feels she is snow.

## *Aubade*

Blessed morning after the storm
waves roll in
each pushing against the next in haste
the dark rolling lake.

White angels—seagulls spread their wings
sail on high. Morning comes striding,
wind tousled, laughing, gilding
each wing, wave and warm bed.

And now
must you leave?

## *Bloodroot Bearings*

The bloodroot thrusts its tender shoots
up through the forest floor rich with acids of leaves
the dark accretions of centuries—mandalas
that repeat each spring just where the footpath
reaches light, near white pines and beeches carved
with the names of lovers.
Snowy corollas tremble in west wind,
silver furry bloodroot stems.

Fragile flowers enfolded in leaves—
coronas, whorls unfurled petals in circles of green
leaves veined with red like the red that runs through
myself and bleeds when I break
the stems staining my hands to remind of kinship
for we have the same needs: sun, rain, food, air.
We are of the same substances that fell
in different combinations.

Yet we are more. I study bloodroot.
The world takes no time to note its harmonious
idiosyncrasies, curious fluted leaves
trefoils that open to dappled light
close with intuitions of night.
Serene go between and compass for my life.
Bloodroot.

## *Meditation*

I am Earth, red sun and yellow flower
and a monarch sipping its sweetness.
We are one great love
knit together:
the spiral tongue, the mountain peaks, the sun.


## *At Palisades Nuclear Power Plant*

Waves lap the sand the sand the sand
and while we keep silence, the silence of Annabelle Lee
a plutonium fuel rod ticks away
stored on the dunes where we used to play.

We played Elephants on a Spider Web
Sword of Damocles
Go Fish.

Peaceful atoms take millennia
to decay.

## *Bats*

Flight of bats
on the rime of night
echo fragile cries
over the still black mirror.
They skim, dip, tip stars
glimmer quicksilver grace
to riffle water.
Swift to kill caddis nymph
lacewing and mosquito in flight;
tilt, soar, glance and glide
insectivores shimmer in the sky loom.

## *The Gatherer*

I gather to me baby scent
the shapes of animals
their colors of fur and feathers,
warmth of sun on water,
taste of thimbleberries on my tongue.
My man, let's roll up in the bear skin
and watch the wheeling stars.
Wild animals flee from you
but while you are away
they come and eat out of my hand.
See quicksilver dapple down through leaves,
sweet odor of forest soaked with rain;
drink these to the core

as I do you.
The green life of the earth turns toward blue light
and is satisfied.
I have domesticated the wild dog,
cultivated wild seeds;
tomorrow I'll invent the wheel.

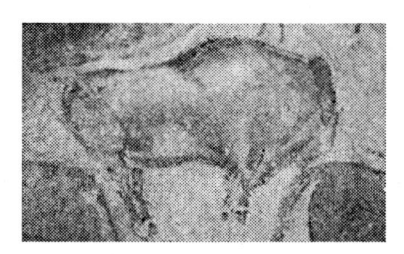

## *The Hunter*

At Altamira
an ancient artist drew
a standing bison.
His hand traced its grace
while his desire for the beast grew
in the flame of the oil lamp.
He painted powerful shoulders,
a sweep of flanks and feet
and the profile of a shaggy head.

The ancient artist knew
the one who created the bison
did so in love
as he drew its reality
in Earth's secret places.

In Utah
an early sculptor incised a mastodon
in the rock with lines sincere
as a child's art.

Lately someone found a Clovis point
in the center of some mastodon bones:
the consummation of an obsessive love.

## *My Deer*

High stepping
clicking
over twigs, leaves, stones
reticent white tail
deer
come near.

Ears, nostrils, eyes
test tense air.
Beware. The wolf
man is here.

Herds of silvery deer
glissade through graveyard greens
eat the flowers in urns.
burn through cool misty air—
all my sly, shadowy deer.
They stamp the sod with
leaf shaped hoof prints.

Today they cross the city street
and some are still concealed
among the grassy dunes.
They draw near...
all my brown-eyed deer.


## *The Effects of Moon Chimes upon Deer and Other Sublunary Beings*

On a quicksilver night
temple chimes speed
from the temple on the moon
and enter in.

I hear music— chimes
high overhead and laughter
and dancing result below.

Deer exalt in the moonlight
twirling, leaping to the music
in the fragrant mown field
on a hot August night.

Moonlight starlight rain down on
rolls of hay, thimbleberries,
tender new rye grass shoots.

Graceful as ever, the moon
chimes through fields of stars—

stars like glass bells.
Below twenty deer glazed
with moonlight, graze
the meadow's silvery grass.

## *The Ancestors*

Far from the otter rocking ocean
that murmurs like a sea turtle's heart
he wanders a waterless prairie.

A schooner pitches on the dark Atlantic
the men, women and children below
have not eaten for days.

Across the empty distance his grandfather
a sturdy bur oak
disappears as he approaches.

Heavy winds lift the vessel—it flies—
the rigging sings with angels
the ancient timbers moan.

Cherokee ponies gallop toward
the foam flecked sea—
his mouth fills with the dust
of moth wings still beating.

At last he slips from this life,
and those who love him and left him behind
guide the airborne ship.

## *Praise*

Praise sun praise air
Praise water praise earth

Praise warm and cold
Praise light and night

Praise solitary moments
Praise community

Praise depths and heights
Praise loon laughter

And moon dappled woods
Praise lady slippers

And praise for jesters
wearing motley

Praise for mothers and fathers
Praise for daughters and sons

Praise for friends
who see us well

Praise teachers and students
Praise painters and poets

Praise for pigment and clay
Praise to spirit guiding hands

Praise ecosystems great and small
from whirling microbes to planetary dances

and Praise to their music
and to the One who set them all in motion.


## *Day Lily*

The day lily comes
carrying its candelabra
of burning candles
wearing its heavenly golden crown
leaping up from the dark leaden base
the tear-drenched ground.

## *My Kites*
## *for my father*

All my tethered kites tremble
cleave the wind with singing
looping, spiraling, weaving
gifts from my father:
heart red, ocean blue
goldfinch yellow
crocus purple
green of
leaping
goat:
s
t
r
i
p
e
s
o
f
J
o
s
e
p
h
's
s
p
  len
    did
      coat

## *On Puget Sound*

Underneath my feet
tangled tree roots feel their way
through clay and a hodge podge of stones
dropped by the glacier that made Puget Sound.

The roots know I am here—
they send the message of me through networks—
travel all the way down to the sound
tell the green kelp.

Kelp forests tell the seals
I admire them and wish to see them soon.
Out in the sound an octopus in her cave
knows I would join her if I could.

And the gray whale I greeted in the Baja last winter
also knows I am here and breaches—
blends its gray with water and sky
so we are all joined in joy.

## *Whale Dreams*

When whales dream
they roam grassy meadows
in their sleep.

In Eden dreamtime one entered
the briny sea
and steered a course by the stars.
All over the world, whales descended into seas.

Now heads down
suspended
great pillars in the deep
they dream then wake

to sing songs that came to them
in sleep...sweet keening songs of
whole earth catapult through liquid halls
enter sea caves, boom through
ships' hulls.
And as the pod moves
from pole to pole they sing their grief

high and low touching places akin
to human souls.

## *Night Realities*

One star trembles on the bottom of the well
candlelight flickers in window glass
the hooting of an owl echoes in the hollow
as my unwinding wishes spin into dreams.


## *La Mer*

Mary's rocking cradle
is the salty sea
the rocking sea is Mary
and Mary is the sea.

## *Lost Found Fawn*

In the thick corn
a whitetail fawn cries out for her mother:
Maaaaa Maaaaa Maaaa.
From the edge of the cornfield we hear
her calling calling
but we can't see her.
Past the corn, a meadow white with
fractals—Queen Anne's Lace—
blue with chicory
all nodding at the sky.
Out of this chaos,
the youngster finds her mom
ruddy in August sun,
they bound away
white flags waving.
Life is good. They feed upon
blueberries and crab apples, thimbleberries
and the corn stalks with small ears.
Repetition and variations
upon the theme
since the time deer
first walked the earth.

## Prairie Child

Prairie flower/prairie flowers
my life blood sown in prairie soil
petals open to the sun
defiant of frost.

Roots twine for miles,
a network that drinks
the least moisture
and gives essence to the land.

Minnesota child, your gaze
was solemn as your hands made
the delicate stitches of the sampler:

you embroidered garlands of flowers,
a little blue dog with a curled tail,
the alphabet cursive and print
(you forgot the J), numerals,
a fancy chair, a row of crowns,
fantastic birds, but not your name.
In the center, 1845 in indigo thread.

As you grew, you were aware of Cherokees,
never far away, your mother's flower garden,
the prairie chicken dancing ground
the flat, blue horizon.

You heard wolves in the distance,
the baaing of sheep
the creak and clang of the windmill.

Prairie flower, pioneer child in a new land,
your fine sewing, my roots.

## *In Darkness*

Under ice under snow
and under the cold
frozen leaf mold
below frost's
unknown
zone

a moonflower seed sleeps
at winter solstice
it waits alone
under earth.
It knows.
Seed.

DNA's secret code
winding inside it
life's mystery
underneath
ice and
snow.

In the deep reach of space
spins a dark twin seed.
Above below
winter snow
both seeds
wait.

## *Birth Control for the Earth Mother Rampant Upon a Fruitful World*

No matter how many times, it is never easy.
She labors over her painting.
Playfully she calls one of them
"Contraction."
She hides her work from male professors
who are aware that art is, after all, female.
It's a secret she knows in her bones, her brain,
her ovaries.

So she hides this under many masks.
The mask series startle visitors to the gallery.
"Artists buy them," she says.

Under the funky clothes she wears,
her breasts float over a white horizon.
She feels her work rising to the top like cream.
With a broad brush she washes layer after layer
of paint that could be primordial ooze.
She lets it happen. The colors flow: burnt sienna,
ultra marine, a glow of vermilion.

Just after Eden she would have squatted
on strong haunches year after year
pushing out babies.
Now she takes the pill.
One child is enough. More than enough.
Each month one or two eggs nest, sigh, die.

Attuned to fecundity, earth, sea, stars,
she paints and the paintings disperse into the world.
Let the dream begin say, with a spill of pearly seeds
from the lush centers of melons or squashes
or swirls of eggs in a teeming sea.
She holds the mystery.
The Earth Mother passes her left hand over her belly
then spatters a loaded brush over the white paper.
The random colors run.

"This is the fun part," she laughs.
"It is the conception."

Later she will labor to bring it to completion.
She pauses to think, brushing her hair away from her brow.
"This is as difficult as giving birth,"
she comments. Then she continues
her painting.

## Sophia's Gold

Her sound unrolls a bolt of star-woven cloth,
Her dance steps the spiral galaxies.

Sophia's signature: the stars, the inner ear,
logos rhythms of nautilus shells, whorled
sunflower centers, DNA.

Sophia, we forgot your light filled flowers—
ancient people carved your name
in caves, upon rock faces.

A young girl dances among coltsfoot—
in the forest a fawn stands for the first time—
mermaid purses wash on shore from the sea.

White milk flows from the golden dome
where the ancient world worshipped:
Hagia Sophia.

A fern bursts through black asphalt,
a nun tends the dying in Calcutta,
an artist designs a rose window,
an unknown composer writes a hymn to Sophia:

Sophia's sound and dance is
turning coltsfoot gold
sun and flower one.

## *Mexico*

## *Ix Chel*

The universe is hers.
She dances before the pyramids
mortared with magic
to the sound of rattles
flutes and drums.

In the forest a diamondback gives birth.
The Mayan throws aerials
spirit of hummingbird
and flower.

Women bring their exceptional gifts:
honeycombs and cloth woven with stories.
The air fills with feathered serpents.

Stars tremble in the cenote still
as she goes on dancing.

## *Dzbilchaltun*
## *(writing on the stone)*

In a chalice shaped pool
where Ix Chel's spirit dreams
three women float free
in water clear, fresh, cool.

Small fish flash like jewels
and white lilies teem
three women in their element
commune in a timeless pool.

Naked on cenote's rim
they dry in sun and wind
three reflections shimmer
on the water's skin.

## *In the Cenote*

Lilies sing silt harmonies.
Listen—they spiral sounds to reeds
that bend to hear.
Unheard by all but the knowing ear,
lilies don't care.

Minnows flash around
their stems—receive the songs
through lateral senses.
Mysterious vibes
stir water, air.

Rivers carry the songs to the sea
where a barely audible hum sustains.
A solar wind carries their songs
to the stars
so all weaves together
in golden threads
in titanium strands.
Gather strength from lilies.

## Copper Canyon and the Tarahumara Indians

The train ride to Copper Canyon is spectacular, Copper Canyon is wild and beautiful, and the inhabitants of Copper Canyon are still living their ancient ways.

Our train trip began in El Fuerte where we boarded the Chihuahua al Pacifico to take us on the train ride of our lives. Soon we were in the wild Sierra Madre Occidental Mountains as the train clattered over the tracks. Up ahead we saw triple switchbacks, tunnels, waterfalls and an occasional village. As we ascended, the green waters in the El Fuerte River below us became crystal clear, and as the train climbed, the cactus studded landscape gave way to tall pines.

At San Rafael we stopped for fifteen minutes and I purchased a couple of finely woven baskets from the Tarahumara Indian women who were standing on the railroad platform with dozens of their baskets. We were now in the Sierra Tarahumara.

The train continued on its zigzag way up the Sierra Madre Tarahumara until we reached our destination. Our hotel, perched on the lip of Copper Canyon, gave us the view of rugged volcanic mountains. From the balcony off of our room we could watch the changing colors of the rocks as the sun went down; later we gazed at a full moon over the canyon and then in the morning we awoke to see great shafts of light shooting over the vastness of Copper Canyon: the changing panorama of cloud and sun over a deep, forested abyss. We could see a network of paths below us made by the Tarahumara Indians who traveled from place to place on foot or with a sure-footed burro.

The Taramuhara who inhabit Copper Canyon's wild habitat have lived here for more than 300 years. They once lived and farmed on the plains but when the Spanish came to colonize their land, they escaped to Copper Canyon where they have lived in freedom ever since. They have preserved their culture in a way other tribes have not been able. Here they could not be conquered since their dwelling places, caves and small huts, were scattered throughout 5,000 square miles of wild country rather than clustered together in a village. They number around 40,000 today, and are adapted to the harsh conditions of the canyon. They know how to use 200 species of plants for food and medicine.

The Jesuits came and taught them Christianity in 1607, then left in the 1700's. They introduced domestic animals such as goats and fruit trees, apple, orange, peach and papaya that are still grown. Left on their own for hundreds of years, these Indians developed unique ways of worshipping. Today the people commemorate Good Friday by killing Judas in effigy to the sound of drums, flutes and hand made violins. Their old beliefs blend with Jesuit teachings. Today there are again Jesuit missions where the people come to worship.

On the steps in front of our hotel the women sat quietly in their colorful hand sewn dresses and hand woven shawls. They sold us their beautiful baskets woven of grasses and pine needles. They are shy and do not even chat among themselves. Some of the women snuggled babies close to them. As they sat, they wove baskets. They also had wooden balls and dolls to sell.

The Tarahumara men are known for their long distance running abilities. Living in the thin air has given them great lung capacity, and they develop stamina by running for sport in Copper Canyon playing a game with a wooden ball and a stick, or running competitive races in teams. They wear sandals with soles cut from rubber tires and held on with leather thongs: they prefer these to modern running shoes.

As hunters, they have been known to hunt a deer by running

after it until the deer drops with exhaustion.

Our trip had a dark side. We learned that living in harmony with the land and each other means everything to the Tarahumara. It is the place where they share with one another in their old traditions. Yet their way of life is threatened: mining operations have polluted some of the streams and logging is stripping the mountains of tall pine and oak. Some believe that deforestation is responsible for the years of drought these subsistence farmers have suffered recently. It would be a loss to the world if these hardy survivors could not continue to live has they have for centuries.

## Tarahumara Newborn

My people say
"Night is the day of the moon."

Full moon tonight over Copper Canyon.
All colors of the moon stream
through the top of my head
my fontanel
open to the sky.

My mother binds me close to her body
in a woolen rebozo.
I can hear her heart beat.
She touches my pulse
on the crown of my head.
Milky way above
sweet milky stream below.

Daybreak now. Cold.
The clouds hold snow but the sun
shoots broad white rays over the canyon.
From the cave where I was born
I see Creation:
a canyon to hide us
ancient footpaths for runners.

I hear fiddles echo off deep canyon walls
drums, flutes, rattles.
Secret ceremonies after my birth,
celebrations of rain
after eight years of drought,

celebrations of sun moon and earth
and of my new life.

Masked dancers with
bells and rattles bond me
to hidden places in
Heaven and Earth.

\*\*\*\*\*\*\*\*

## *My Baby*

I watched my baby grow rosy
as she leaped into this life,
drew air.

A soft breeze moved living leaves
the sun spilled liquid gold—
neutrinos through the trees.

Waking, my baby raised her head
and smiled at the dancing green.
Her bright eyes saw
green with gold spilled through
and bits of Heaven breaking
all around us.

It was such a long journey
and now she is here.
She feels my warm breath
close to her ear.

## Queen Asa's Viking Ship

The Viking ship sails north,
its keel hisses over the sea as
Queen Asa and her slave girl
embark on their journey.

The water clear, the air pure
the steering paddle starboard guides them
past the lung of the sea.

Only yesterday they passed cave bear
elk and reindeer
carved in rock faces along Norway's coast
then human figures, horned, dancing
Bronze Age sun wheels, trumpets
and phallic weapons of war.
Frozen in an Ice Age, iron hammers
magical runes, grave stones set in earth
outline a sailing ship with rich brooches
and silver vessels in its hold.

They passed an age of gold: entwined dragons
set with precious stones
ornaments for people
and horses.

Now through the glass see
Queen Asa's dragon ship
flow on the water that purls below
as they pass over beyond Thule.

## *Refuge*

The beach seagull lovely
surf sand painting the shore
I slept on the sand
washed in wave sounds
and awoke to find myself covered
with ladybugs.

These bright orange insects sought
refuge in me
as if I were driftwood
sand
or a tree.


## *Variations*

One star trembles
on the bottom of the well.

Candlelight flickers
in window glass.

The hooting of an owl
echoes in the hollow

and my unwinding wishes
spin into dreams.

# Islands in the Galapagos Archipelago

## What Charles Darwin Saw

When we arrived in the Galapagos Islands the first part of March, the rainy season, their endemic species were at their best, wearing their courting regalia, showing off, dancing. We had no trouble seeing this happen since unlike other places in the world, the long isolated Galapagos' wildlife do not fear humans.

The mature male of the blue footed boobie attracts a mate with his cerulean blue legs and feet. As if this were not enough, he offers her a stick in his large bill, holding it high in the air while dancing on his gorgeous blue legs.

Hard to resist this!

The male of the frigate bird usually is not into courtship this early, but when we visited, they were courting to make up for El Nino last year that caused their nesting to be unsuccessful in some cases. The handsome black frigate bird has a brilliant red pouch on his neck he inflates to attract a mate. Once she chooses one, he covers her eyes with his wings. He doesn't want her to see any gaudy competitors in the vicinity. And there were many riding the air currents on their scimitar shaped wings and perching in the trees.

On these volcanic islands walking is sometimes difficult: jagged lava underfoot is harsh and one must be careful not to step on iguanas or bird nests. The trusting inhabitants of the Galapagos do not move out of the way of humans. We were careful not to disturb them.

The males of the marine iguanas on Santa Cruz were at their best wearing beautiful red and green mottled lizard skin outfits solely to attract the opposite sex. We were surprised to see that the marine iguanas on other islands wore basic black. They blended in with the black lava where they sunned themselves en masse. Why the Santa Cruz marine iguanas evolved in a different way is a question Charles Darwin pondered. It still fascinates.

On other islands, the green sea turtles were converging to mate in the water and lay their eggs on land. The sea was full of the huge green sea turtles. At night the females made landings on the sandy beaches to lay eggs. We saw their tracks in the sand and were careful not to encroach on the places where their eggs lay buried under the equatorial sun.

The female of the Galapagos hawk is fierce and devious. The mating is done high in the air and afterwards she drives the male away. She may then mate with four or five other males. Since they all think they are the father, they all provide food for the new hatchlings. These fledglings come in to the world well provided for.

We loved frolicking in the water with the California sea lions. They may look awkward on land, but as we peered through our diving masks, we could see their grace under water. They peered back at us with curiosity

On land the female and juvenile sea lions go where they wish. The male stakes out territory on a beach and defends it against other males. We saw some males with deep wounds on their necks and backs. The property owner mates with whatever female arrives on his beach. In spite of these encounters, the sea lions seem to live a rather joyful life, playing and leaping in the water, then lazily sunning themselves.

We also saw the smaller Galapagos seal and the penguins who made their way to the Galapagos Islands on a cold sea current and established colonies there. The penguins whizzed through the water like small torpedoes. The marine iguanas used their long tails to propel themselves through the waves to feed upon algae.

Underwater the tropical fishes were going through their mating and bonding rituals as they passed our snorkeling masks along with a few sharks, but these fish were too numerous for us to sort out. They were a colorful kaleidoscope.

The Galapagos Islands are famous for their several species of huge land tortoises. We saw them migrating in the wild on their large elephant like legs. In the past, whaling ships and pirates wiped out some species of the gentle giants by gathering them for food on long sea journeys.

We felt lucky to witness these primal rites in this Eden-like place.

# *Overboard*

The sea brims with moonlight—
a host of night flying gulls
trail their long slender tails—
ghostly past our ship.

Starboard the Southern Cross hangs
just above the horizon.
In deep labyrinths below
blooms the black coral.
Everyone knows you must not pluck it
though some have tried.

All caught in a maze
between visible and unseen...

I fall into dark warm brine—
moved here and there where
equatorial currents converge.

I descend past shark eyes shining
in watery moonlight
down the warm sea column—
something brushes my inner thigh—

a cloud of opalescent diatoms
spin in moonshine.
Slowly I rise to breathe fresh air.

I cry out in the wake of two hundred
frolicking dolphins—
common dolphins, I'm told.


## *Floreana*

No human habitation on Floreana.
Humans go mad here—
odor of sulfur in the air—
our cameras stop.
I touch the clean white skull
bone of a seal polished by ghost
crabs by wind and wave.

Floriana, pink with flamingos
green sea turtle eggs
incubate in warm sand.
Life hangs in the balance at
creation's way station.

It's time to go
yet we take one last stroll
down a dazzling beach of sand
where two sea lions doze.

There be talismans here
left by pirates and hikers
on a driftwood log:
sea polished bones
at the end of a trail…

and so I leave what the sea has left:
the innermost spiral of a shell.


## *Isla Espanola*

Tectonic plates float like cream
on a sea of milk...
yet the sea can no longer douse fire.
When plates collide, archipelagos arise.
One by one the Galapagos arose from the sea.

Isla Espanola the first
to burst from earth's molten core,
from the sea floor
where tectonic plates collide
molten rock spews.

Walk with me on Isla Espanola.
The volcano is quiet now.
Be careful not to stumble on the rocks.
Watch out for the lava lizards.

Below us, aquamarine waves bash
hard black basalt
boom through blow holes—
lava tubes interlace the volcanic
island's base. Long Pacific rollers
burst into powerful white fountains.

Indolent marine iguanas glitter like obsidian

spear points, wear Caliban's spiky armor
cling to rocks with their long spear like toes
swim the sea with dragonish candor.

Handsome black and white masked boobies
guard their eggs and chicks on high cliffs.
A frenzied flock of noddy terns
fold their wings and plunge from sky to
sea like daggers.

Espanola, island in the Galapagos Archipelago
where Gaia's forces meet: tectonic plates
sun, wind, gravity spin, sea currents
rain, seeds, eggs
land and sea changes to malleable lives:
a curious miraculous menagerie.

*******

## *Where Have All the Goddesses Gone?*

When Mother Eve fell from grace
Massacio's Adam turned his face.

When Artemis' bow lost its sting
all the satyrs flooded in.

After Ix Chel's temple fell
hotels sprang up on Cozumel.

With Demeter despised, shunned
residual poisons leave us stunned.

With Aphrodite degraded, mocked
the porno business leaves us shocked.

With Sophia's radiance lost
can we continue to bear the cost?

## *Hieros Gamos*

On the way to Egypt
two lions bound in the dark
across level Earth.

The maned lion chases the lioness
and she stays ahead.

They carry desert
Nile and fertile delta.
They carry the royal sphinx.

Inside of them are the sun
and the darkness
of Africa.

Inside of the are the
four directions
and the center.

## Holy Bones

Under this dome of white bone
nothing.

Down my xylophone spine
no telegraph.

My pelvis an empty saddle.
My articulated arms legs hands feet
silent as stone.

My bones.
The wind plays through
this temple of bones.


## Agate, A Gate

Go to the beach at Grand Marais
to watch the small stones roll.

Surf slants in
licks and slicks and clicks the stones
sometimes casts up bones
and out and in again:
black, brown, bronze Lake Superior stones,
pudding, Petoskey, quartz,, greenstone, copper.
Folded carnelian, amethyst, jasper, opal.

So choose a stone made of star stuff
a rosy stone veined with blue—
maybe you'll find the stone is a gate
when held to the setting sun.

## The Green Man's Secret

I peered at his face of oak leaves:
body, arms, legs, feet
all leaf and vine, vegetable green.

"Take my hand," the green man said
in his leafy voice. I held his knarled hand—
he led me through the starry night.

The air filled with long tailed moths—
fireflies blinked their cold light
I heard the buzz of locusts ringing in the night.

He led me to my father's grave where
deer grazed moonlit grass
and then felt a stare,

I saw myself in a deer's eye
as in a dome of glass
his antlers dropped as branches

when the season passed
and sprouted velvet buckhorns
when song birds sang at last.

"All things are made new!"
I shouted in great relief.
"Yes," the green man said: "I releaf."

He took me home then
as the sun rose over the hill.
I saw two brown foxes playing:
I saw that all is well.

## *Dark Rib Ride*

Shadows of cottonwood seeds fly
swift flickers ride dune ribs upward
updrafts catch as
azure bleeds to ultramarine.

I am the shadow of a narwhal
never captured alive
on ribs of ocean floor

the shadows of impalas pursued
by the spotted cheetah
the bounding shade under
belly and paws.

Tumble, tremble the cottonwood leaves
the full moon casts shadows
dancing and mute.
The black ribs of buttes

lengthen in desert sands.
My dark twin rests in deep cool canyons
free beyond all apple dreams.

## *Shopping for a Drum*

Some heavy drums had bark
and some had fur from unknown animals
and one lovely Michigan drum, I was told
would balance my chakras.

Its sound resonated through me.
Hmmmm. My chakras
seem to be okay.

I shook rattles and shuffled around the shop
while the clerk pretended
not to see.

Then I found a noise
so exquisitely piercing and clear
it could cause Ezekiel to rise—
to rise and dance. Dance Ezekiel dance.
And may I have the next dance?

And while dancing
I'll play my hand made bell
from Cameroon. Not your hum-drum drum
but forged in a furnace and shaped
into an iron throat fastened
to a wooden handle that fits my hand well.

There is a stick to bang on it
fastened with a hemp rope.
I believe my Cameroon bell will be heard on Earth
and other dimensions as well.

## *Denali Spring Time*

Drip
Drip
Drip
Drip
Arctic ice loses its grip.

Virgin ferns bow modestly
only wait for bird songs
to unfold them.

In its bed of stone
the stream slips away to sea
whispering secrets of egg and bone.

Frogs long suspended in brittle sleep
frozen to the core
as stiff as little glass jugs or
clergy collars or petrified wood
unable to give or get hugs
now leap
resurrected by love.

Wood frogs dapper
and dappled in sleek green suits
leap into Denali spring time
where still water reflects
the blues, the greens, everything.

Dimpled, dappled renewed like the moon
frogs crouch under ferns—ferns

still wearing fuzzy bronze coats
bursting earth with clenched fists
then unfurling among millions of violets.

Bees meander and hum their songs of honey
while joyous frog choruses
sing all night of love
moon beams and mud.


## *Canadian Geese*

Fat with summer's grasses
Stuffed with Saskatchewan corn

Veed geese weave the windy reaches
Gabble green speech and

Cascade away.

## He Was a Farm Boy Once

Thrown just so, skipping stones
can walk on water,
and once I thought he could too.
With his jack knife
he could fashion a willow whistle
from a branch at water's edge,
carving, tapping the bark to loosen it
from the sappy stick.
When I go visit my father
this spring
will he skip stones for me?
Or make a willow whistle for me?

## Wild Flowers

Please take these flowers I never picked:
blue lupine from open
meadows
harebells from
clefts of fractured rock,
violets in tufts
from sun dappled woods
rue anemone in umbels—
blue and white to mirror sky.

I leave them rooted to acid soil
shy essences.

Know these are my sky blue wishes
I would give to you
but never will.


## *High School Library*

I peer into the rectangle of glass
to observe schools of students
drifting among the stacks,
nibbling the edges of books.
The bold ones command the center space
the quiet ones lurk in study carrels and
circumvent the center aisles.

I observe their eddies of movement,
the interplay of dominances, sudden disquiets
and momentary alert silences.
The dream of wild rivers
lies in back of their eyes.
I tap on the glass with my fingers;
they turn and stare with pineal eyes.

## *Wordless Song*

As we gaze into a still woodland lake
the sun burns the mist away
and all around us
night birds turn their heads
slowly dreaming.

Breaking our reflection,
a water moccasin weaves
his wordless song on water.
See him sink
below our understanding again.


## *Foggy Dawn*

The mourning doves four
notes brocade the fog horn's two
hoots weaving first day of summer leaves.

Song birds chant matins
sweet mathematical spires of song.
I wake to praise of mourning doves on the wing
they whirr the air
they have hidden their young
in a twiggy nest on a ledge somewhere.

The orioles dangle their hanging basket
amid a leafy tangle over the sidewalk where

it sways with each breeze. Unaware
of orange miracles in mid air
people stroll below it.

Song sparrows peek in our window
pecking at phantom assailants.
Robins carry fat green worms into the hedge.
Purple martins twitter recalling
summer fairs with birds on strings
for children to spin in giddy circles.

Of one mind one hundred herring gulls rise
from the sand, into dazzling air, sky dancing,
wind riding, descending to scoop silver flashes
from the slowly rolling waves.

## *Bonesounds*

Make my left thigh bone a flute—
punch holes for fingers and lips.

Make my skull a drum—
beat on the bone with sticks.

Of my jointed finger bones
string wind chimes
so breezes may click them
outside your bedroom window.

To humor the wave length unwinding me,
make the sound no bell tolls
no wood thrush knows
no human tongue tells.

## *The Monarchs' Wedding*

Paired dancers robed in saffron
striped with black
burn like tigers
pulse bright blue air.

Eight wings tango
black downy bodies clasp tight
one wings upright
one rides below with folded wings.

Delight and symmetry
in the chaos
they might cause.
In Mexico a storm cloud spirals.

## Song in the Flesh

My body tells me
I was meant to be what I am:
procreator and nourisher of life.
The life of the mind is proud,
seeks commendation
is not satisfied.

Spirit and flesh are one in me.

All life streams through me:
I am all women and all men.
I am the children, the grasses, the stars.
The sea sounds in me.
In the mountains I shout and leap and dance.
My breath commingles with the wind blown leaves
and my imprint is eternal.

## Radial Lines

Radial lines, intersections, chance meetings
Patterns running from the still center
Harmonies, lines, circles, ripples
A stone thrown in a still pool
Endless concentric circles
Sound waves speeding
Through the universe
Planets spinning

Sun blessing all
Be still
Know


## *Sophia's Sound*

First a great sound—a sound
that broke upon
chaos
then there were all
all all all
and when Sophia's sound
a great low loving vowel
and then all vowels
opened earth air sea fire
and life began.
"Do not fear Eve," said she.

Birds of the air
and serpents in the sea
man woman
and progeny.

# *Mist*

White mist rises from the harbor—
farther upstream it slides
all around the reeds
around the islands.

The river sings today
as it runs through our town
on its way to the sweetwater seas
on its way to the Gulf of St. Lawrence
on its way to the wild dark Atlantic.

From the bridge I can see
October's first frost dissipate
in Sunday morning sun light.
Prickly seed pods of moon flowers burst
upon sandy loam.
Cloudy milt and coral eggs
cling to stream bed stones.

Glory surrounds us like water—
we sense it and see it.
We feel its hot and cold
its colors its sounds
as the river sings its songs of salmon
as it runs to the sea and rises sunward.

With locators sure as salmon
we will return.

## Dark Energy

The dark universe exhales—
unknowing we go about our lives,
babies born, people die.
We yearn for them.
In our hearts we know

there breathes a oneness:
the earth, the stars, beyond.
Those we love we will see again.
No limits. None.

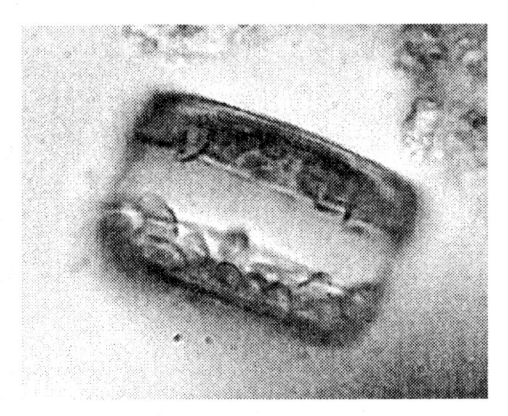

## Unseen Opals

Life on Earth loves
her opal jewel boxes
unseen extravaganzas strewn
from sunlight, bedrock and water
to amplify the very air.

## Great Lakes Give and Take

These lakes hold gifts and treasures—
shining fish of rose gold and silver
all bespangled and glittering emerald shiners.
These freshwater seas slide Atlanticward
and flow forever in sea dreams.

Eagles and swift peregrines ride their airstreams.
Beaches of quartz sand rise and
beaches where agates tumble and slide.

The Niagara escarpment rises above
glittering embayments.
Burbot and whitefish dart depths among
bones of sailors who went down with their ships.

Moody and fickle
they chuckle and lap
turn sullen and black they take back
and give and then take back.
Take back.

## *Great Lakes Imprint On Us*

Leave the Great Lakes?
Never.
We feel their pulse in our blood,
in our sinews, our bones.
vibrations in our bellies.
Their islands arise in waking dreams.
And even in sleep we know
moon, stars and planets float in their waters
until dawn.

The Great Lakes gulp the sun at noon
while diatom symphonies
dazzle green currents
and curious protozoa graze.
In silent depths below
lie burbot, sturgeon, lake trout.

White sailboats belly out in the breeze.
On the beach rare piping plovers
hide their nests among stones.
We walk through singing sands,
scoop pails of water,
build spirit castles of wet sand.
Then we brush sand from our feet
and our hands.
The lakes' imprint is in us.

## *Great Yin Mother*

We're trolling for trolls or silver salmon
for anything below our quivering lines
we hold taut and eager. The dark yin mother dances
over small salmon and gives us one small king leaping.
Rocking to on fro on her thighs
the motor mutters low.
At Palisades, a plutonium tomb
perches on the dune.
Once a toddler seeing Lake Michigan
for the first time dreamily called it "milk."
Great milk mother tumbling with fossils of ancient whales
and corals, the ribs of sunken ships where fish dream.
As she loves to do, the yin mother plays crest and
trough—Her sweetwater laughter laps us, and as we tumble
in her lap her laughter splashes shore away—sand dunes
collapse; the sunny wooded dunes where we once played
crumble before Yin's fluid grace. The droll mother
juggles bones, trees, ancient roof beams.
And what of a cask of plutonium?
It's all the same.

## *Snowy Owls*

Silent as silk they float
through tamaracks and dying oaks
then perch in the crown of a pine.
Starfall and moonglow
light their white down.

Their yellow eyes pierce the woods
quite near the cemetery
where many friends are lain.

Snowy owls hear
a whisker twitch, a leaf blow
across the tunneled forest floor.
Warm blooded lives tremble
below.

The owls hear
and stoop to prey.

## To Daughters and Sons

First a fish with fins and gills
   I swam in a little sea.

I heard the boom and swish
   my mother's tide
then passed through an arduous time.

      I was blue.
      I cried.

Comfort me with the sound of the sea.

## *The Entryway*

I'll not enter that back door again,
pass the denim clothes
hung on pegs
and the speckled gray
wash basin, pitcher and roller towel
on the wall
of that narrow passageway.

And I'll not see her in this life again.
She always met me at the door smiling
so glad to see me after many years.
Her blue eyed, white furred kittens

won't come mewing to the entryway
where she fed them cream
table scraps
left over coffee.

My grandmother with eyes as blue as
forget-me-nots
that sparkled when she tilted

her head to say, "How?"
She couldn't hear as well as when
she was young.

Now she has gone—
she always welcomed me
at the entry.

## *Equation*

Never fear death.
You can't kill her
with swords or guns.
She is life returning
in myriads of forms
colors and sounds
beyond us now.

When the last breath goes out
the body sighs
the spirit releases out
into the ethereal and
it finds wisdom
unknown on earth.

Life is sweet:
death the sweetest knowing of all.

# *Africa*

## *In a Nyala's Eye*

The rain bird utters
bell like notes.
Nearby elephants fan their ears
and seldom sleep.

Fragrance of acacia trees sweeps
over us as we sleep
in the Lebombo Mountains.

Callings of birds and animal herds
sweet Zulu harmonies
insistent drumming
pulses through the trees,
the streams—our blood.

## *At Victoria Falls*

Through mist moist air,
I hand a deaf man a coin and hear
the fall's majestic roar.

White water falls over black basalt
scours rock, splits bone,
carves logs, Shona hones.

Mist rises, rainbows arc over
deep gorge waters below
hollows stone—
whirlpools slowly turn
looking deep

Shona know the dragon home—a labyrinth
of coiled power below.
So above its chaos, soaked to the core,

I climb slippery stairs,
I follow a path.
Look, on forest floor a
green mamba's tongue boldly
samples Zambezi damp air.

Red sun bird, rain bird's bell like song
elephant herds, a shy spotted water buck
bounds away from me—a dappled song
in the shady rain forest.

Don't walk the path below—

        crocodiles lie in
     blue lilies, and Jesus birds
    walk unconcerned. All around
are hippo snouts hippo eyes and hippo ears.

   Blood red sun goes down on my left
a moon full of gold blooms on my right—
    this is my post card I never sent
       I carry it in my bones.

## *I Still Hear the Roar of the Falls*

Full moon aflame over the Zambezi River

glows in crocodile eyes
shines on whiskers of leopards
who prowl not far away.

Moon on my left
the sun on my right
left moments ago.
Zambezi waters gather and
fall over dark basalt to rise again
as moon rainbows...
all is rainbow to the bone.

Zulu warriors sing a cappella
and where will they sleep tonight?
Their voices sun bird
and rain bird
violet chested roller
and profound sounds of the falls.

Unearthly harmonies rise
wet the jungle with sudden rain
wet the savannah
touch places where lions sleep.

Rhythms embedded in tribal rituals
and drums respectful
of the Mother giving grains, ores
and little children.

Playful elephants come to feed
upon sweet amaretto bark
then leave a splintered landscape
in their wake.

Baboons play on the rooftops
and look both ways before crossing the street
while beggars hold out their hands.

The poorest people on Earth make
the loveliest music of all.

## Riding the Spirit Elephant

Today I rode an elephant—
always knew I would.

The elephant's name was Emily—
she carried me and a Zimbabwean man
over the grassy plains.

"We treat the elephants with kindness here,"
he said, and I could see it was so.

Emily, sweet and playful, stole
leaves with her trunk
from an elephant nearby
and waved her huge leafy ears.

Her rolling gait carried us over
a tawny sea of grass; her huge legs
kept a steady dream like pace.

She tested the stream bottom we crossed
with her great round feet.

From the elephant's back I gazed
at the blue sweep of African sky,
I heard the calls of African birds,
saw gentle giraffes
felt the presence of lions nearby.

Years ago I knew this would happen-
I still don't know how or why.

\*\*\*\*\*\*\*

## *Seaspeak*

"Lie beside me
in the moon light
relaxed as a sleeping
seal. Let me sweep you
with seaweed green as spinach
sea lettuce mottled and leathery
whips of kelp, potsherds, shells, algae
and I'll open my delicate secrets to you."

That's what the ocean spoke to me.
Inside of me drumming deep blue rhythms,
the sounding sea poured into my whole body
all my five senses and senses I never perceived before:
"Fear neither land nor sea nor any thing living or dead:
Do not fear the universe," the wise, wide and deep sea said.

## *Abyss*

I take a deep breath and descend
dreaming of wells
and whales in a midnight sea,
of a dragon's foot in the bedrock.
A bird sings long before dawn.
I ascend
wearing lapis lazuli
of deepest blue shot through with gold
and walk a road strewn with black walnuts.
Trillium in profusion bloom around the trees.

Divine children walk and talk at birth—
I dance with a child in my arms
dance away from demons and thieves.

We see through green glasses,
we hike in sturdy shoes.
People we don't even know stand in the wings
to watch our ragtime dance.

Venus blazes its shining pathway on the sea
narwhals, male and female
rise side by side to greet us.

## *Dawn Dragons*

Dawn dragons fly over
town, dunes, lake
to swallow the swollen moon
that baroque pearl rolled
down to shimmering brink of sky.

In cool pursuit
hordes of Tao Dragons stride
glide quicksilver golden
just roused from the China Sea
to eat the teasing moon.

## *Mount St. Helens Blooms*

Hidden in the folds of her skirt,
safe under mountain,
under pumice
under glassy ash

pocket gophers
deep in tunnels
pop up
to bring seeds
from underneath.
Toothy survivors in upper air.

No one thought anything
could grow
after the blast, the lava flow,
after the toxic gases, and
the ashes.

Just look at the foxglove now,
the ox eyed daisies, rugged pioneers,
the lupine, tansy, red alder.
Even the Roosevelt elk have
decided to return.

## *Basic Instincts*

Goslings follow the leader—
waddling after an imprint.

Veed geese fly home
the arctic tern,
the hummingbird,
and bright eyed warblers
fly to their tropical havens.
Lake trout swirl at river mouths
then race upstream.
American eels return from the sea
to freshwater streams.

Undersea
lobsters march in single file—
they know exactly where

they are going.
And we humans also know
where we are going

God's green imprint is
upon our hearts.

## *Jonah's Journey*

Jonah, never the captain of his fate,
wanted control and ran from God's command,
yet God holds all in the palm of His hand.
Jonah slept through a storm— hid in great dread.
Then his shipmates cast lots—headed toward land,
"Just throw me in I may as well be dead."
The deep dark ocean rolled over his head.

A great fish gulped him—he was in despair—
after three dark nights Jonah breathed fresh air.
He waited for wicked Ninevah's destruction
but it was he who needed instruction,
as the Lord chose to forgive not destroy.
Another hard earned lesson for our boy.

# *Eric Our Guide Shows Us Santa Croce*

Santa Croce is a giant ear,
grief haunted cathedral—
Byzantine keeper of secrets and the bones
of great ones under its stones.
And I who longed for Florence
felt suddenly so unsure
standing on chancy ground all unprepared for

that loud sound
so organic and low—
does it emanate from now
or from long ago?

Strange vibrations
hum through cavernous air
and as I stood near Michelangelo's tomb
with three sad sweet muses
each hair on my body rose
when Eric said,

"Michelangelo is not buried in the tomb
but under the floor"…I knew
his ghost brushed me then
as we lingered there.
Florence never treated her great ones well.

Circling left
("The Inquisition started here," Eric
mentions in passing)
pass Giotto's tender frescos of St. Francis.

A celestial clock above the door
points to heaven
with one hand—we stand below.
Dante was sure the circles below us
held many Florentines.

And though Dante's sarcophagus inside is empty
his statue at the entrance stares over the square—
his demeanor seems to say: "the Inferno is here—
is everywhere."

## *Dante's Limerick*

In Florence the banning of books
caused Dante to say, "Gadzooks!
if I wanted an Inferno
I would have used Sterno
like sensible outdoor cooks."

## Twin Sewing Lessons

Rachel and Vanessa are sewing—
sewing for rag doll and teddy bear.

Rag doll is resplendent in gold sequins
white square buttons, bright
blue beads sewn with care onto red felt.

Vanessa holds her needle in her right hand,
Rachel holds hers in her left.
They sit across the table
from each other, perfectly mirrored.

They sew ribbons and buttons and sequins
on a hat fit for the queen.
White teddy bear has a circle skirt
rimmed in gold sequins.
Rag doll and teddy bear are going to a ball.

The girls are sprouting new front teeth
and they dream of perfect beauty as
they sew patches and hearts
to repair damages.

They tie knots and thread needles
chatting all the time over their
pleasant work as women
all over the world have done—
since time began.

## *Forget Me Nots and Otters*

We paddle—our canoe winds
between banks of blue flowers
and luscious
ferns laced with dragon flies
the river of forget me nots and otters.

We've been on other rivers:
the St. Mary's in a leaky boat,
the Pine in a canoe,
the wide Zambezi above Victoria Falls,
the Rio Grande rafting rapids...
rivers slow and rivers wild.

But on the river of forget me nots
dark water dreams its way
while we steer around

deadheads, and low branches.
Our seven year old grandson is with us
on this rainless day
delighted to be amid blue flowers
ferns, and dragonflies.
He expects to see a dinosaur soon.

Our granddaughter age five
is in the other canoe
between her mom and dad.
She wants to wade in the water—
she wants to wiggle her toes in mud.
We paddle immersed in bird songs,

butterflies and clouds of
blue forget me nots.

## *The Gift of Rabbit*

Remember the time
you ran down a young rabbit
for me?
Zigzagging through the field
predator and prey.
You didn't kill it, you cradled it.
Your hearts beat fast
and you carried it to me—
you carried the soft rabbit
between your shirt and warm skin.
You stood laughing
as the bunny burrowed into
your clothes.

No one ever gave me a rabbit before.
I took it home.
I let it go.

*Some of these poems have been published in other collections*

"The Gatherer" won Best of the Year on the *Grape Poetry Website.*

*Grand Valley Review,* published by Grand Valley State University, published "Where Have All the Goddesses Gone?" vol X, Spring 1994. "Birth Control for The Earthmother Rampant Upon a Fruitful World," "Sophia's Gold," "Circuits," "Wolfman."

"Bear Woman" won *Writer's Digest* top 100 in 1988

"At Palisades Nuclear Power Plant" won first place Oakland Community College Poetry Contest.

Snowbound Writers Contests: first place "Bear Woman"; second place: "Ix Chel"; third place "Lake Michigan Aubade."

*Art/Life a hand made publication* published "Canadian Geese," "The Gatherer," "North," "Ix Chel."

Midwest Poetry Festival, 1983, *A Publication of the Society of Midwest Literature* published "Bear Woman," "North," "To Sons and Daughters," "Dark Rib Ride," "The Hunter."

*Gusto*, 1981, "North."

*Sky,* Winter 92/93 published "At Palisades Nuclear Power Plant."

*The 2RiverView* published "The Hero's Journey" and "Hieros Gamos," Spring 2000.

*The Lunar Archives*, a website devoted to fractals, prose and poetry commissioned the Galapagos and Africa poems and has published other poems and art.

*PW Review*, an online poetry magazine published "Bear Woman," "Summer Solstice," " Two Horses," "Maybe the Manitous," " Refuge," "Variations," " Lost Found Fawn" and "On Puget Sound."

*Snakeskin*, an on line poetry magazine in the United Kingdom, published "Where Have All the Goddesses Gone?"

*Pigs 'n Poets,* an online magazine from the University of Wisconsin Oshkosh, published "The Hunter"and "The Gatherer."

*Gumball Poetry,* an on line magazine of art and poetry published in Portland, Oregon, published "Wolfman" in their first issue. *Gumball* also dispenses poems along with gumballs in gumball machines.

*Artvilla,* an online magazine of music, art and poetry, published the haiku "Frog Pond," as well as *Michigan Natural Resources* magazine.